CORNERSTONES OF FREEDOM™

THE UNDERGROUND RAILROAD

BY LUCIA RAATMA

CHILDREN'S PRESS®

An Imprint of Scholastic Inc.

New York Toronto London Auckland Sydney

Mexico City New Delhi Hong Kong

Danbury, Connecticut

Content Consultant
James Marten, PhD
Professor and Chair, History Department
Marquette University
Milwaukee, Wisconsin

Library of Congress Cataloging-in-Publication Data
Raatma, Lucia.
  The Underground Railroad/by Lucia Raatma.
     p. cm.—(Cornerstones of freedom)
  Includes bibliographical references and index.
  ISBN-13: 978-0-531-25043-3 (lib. bdg.)   ISBN-10: 0-531-25043-1 (lib. bdg.)
  ISBN-13: 978-0-531-26568-0 (pbk.)   ISBN-10: 0-531-26568-4 (pbk.)
  1. Underground Railroad—Juvenile literature. 2. Fugitive slaves—United
States—History—19th century—Juvenile literature. 3. Antislavery
Movements—United States—History—19th century—Juvenile
literature. I. Title. II. Series.
  E450.R145 2011
  973.7'115—dc22   2011009493

1 2 3 4 5 6 7 8 9 10 R 21 20 19 18 17 16 15 14 13 12

Photographs © 2012: age fotostock/The Print Collector: 13; Alamy Images:
29 (Everett Collection Inc.), 42 (Kevin Parsons); AP Images: 6, 16, 26,
44, 46, 49 (North Wind Picture Archives), 30 (Ahn Young-joon); Corbis
Images/Hulton-Deutsch Collection: cover; Getty Images: 10 (Father
Browne/Universal Images Group/Hulton Archive), 4 top, 15 (MPI); Library
of Congress: 23, 50; Lucia Raatma: 64; National Archives and Records
Administration/National Park Service/Frederick Douglass National Historic
Site: 22; National Geographic Stock/Jerry Pinkney: 8; NEWSCOM/Scripps
Howard News Service: 40 (Levi Coffin House Association), 54 (Lori King/
The Toledo Blade); North Wind Picture Archives: 12; Ohio Historical
Society: 37, 56 top; Superstock, Inc.: 39 (Everett Collection), 36 (Image
Asset Management Ltd.), 18 (Edmond Morin/Collection of Archiv for Kunst
& Geschichte, Berlin), 43 (Steve Vidler); The Granger Collection, New
York: 2, 3, 19 (Eastman Johnson), 24 (Theodor Kaufmann), 38 (James L.
Langridge), 20 (Thomas Moran), 47 (George Richmond), 48, 58 (A.R. Waud),
4 bottom, 5 bottom, 5 top, 14, 27, 28, 31, 32, 33, 51, 57, 59; The Image Works:
41, 56 bottom (Mary Evans Picture Library), 34 (ullstein bild), back cover
(Jim West).

Did you know that studying history can be fun?

BRING HISTORY TO LIFE by becoming a history investigator. Examine the evidence (primary and secondary source materials); cross-examine the people and witnesses. Take a look at what was happening at the time—but be careful! What happened years ago might suddenly become incredibly interesting and change the way you think!

Contents

Slavery in the United States

Black Africans were forcibly brought to America to work as slaves as early as 1619.

In the 1600s, people came to the American colonies to start a new life. They hoped to experience freedom and escape the restrictions of the English government. But as the colonies grew and then formed a new nation in the 1700s, the practice of slavery also grew.

Slave traders brought African men, women, and children to the Americas. These slaves were forced to do hard labor for no pay. The first slaves came to Jamestown, Virginia, in 1619. By 1808, it was illegal to bring slaves from Africa, but the practice continued illegally.

When the country's founders wrote the **U.S. Constitution** in 1787, they struggled with the idea of slavery. Benjamin Franklin was president of an **abolitionist** society that had been formed in Philadelphia, Pennsylvania, in 1775. Wealthy landowners George Washington and Thomas Jefferson, however, both owned slaves.

By the 1800s, the economy of the South depended on slave labor to work large **plantations** with crops such as cotton and tobacco. As years passed, some states outlawed slavery. They were known as free states. The states that continued to allow the practice were known as slave states.

Enslaved African Americans longed to be free, and some tried to escape to free states. In 1793, the U.S. Congress passed the first **Fugitive** Slave Act. This law required the return of any slaves who escaped to another U.S. state or territory. The law also made it illegal to help runaway slaves.

Despite the law, abolitionists often helped slaves escape. One way they did this was through a system that was known as the Underground Railroad.

CHAPTER 1

HOW THE UNDERGROUND RAILROAD WORKED

Freed or escaped slaves often helped other slaves to freedom along the Underground Railroad.

THE UNDERGROUND RAILROAD

is a term used for the secret network of people and places that assisted fugitive slaves as they escaped. Most slaves were running from owners in the South and heading to free states. This system was most active in the 20 to 30 years leading up to the American Civil War (1861-1865). The busiest parts of the network were near the regions that bordered slave states, making the Ohio River the center of the activity.

Slaves were brought to the Americas aboard overcrowded ships, which were dirty and disease-ridden.

Understanding the Name

The Underground Railroad was not literally a railroad, and it was not underground. Instead, it was an informal system of people and safe places that enabled slaves to move in secret.

There are several stories regarding the origin of its name. According to one, in 1831, a slave named Tice Davids escaped from Kentucky and swam across the Ohio River. With the help of abolitionists, he hid and made his way to Sandusky, Ohio. When Davids's owner looked for him, just across the Ohio River, he is said to have thought that the slave "must have gone off on an underground railroad."

Another story says that slave hunters in Pennsylvania came up with the term. A third version says that a slave explained making his way north where "the railroad ran underground all the way to Boston."

Abolitionist Beliefs

Leaders of the abolitionist movement created the Underground Railroad. Quakers, who are members of a religious group called the Religious Society of Friends, were the first organized abolitionists. They strongly believed that slavery was not in keeping with their Christian principles. By the early 1800s, every state in the North had ended slavery. Abolitionist ideas then spread west into territories that later became Indiana and Ohio. Many abolitionists also viewed slavery as the complete

A VIEW FROM ABR⭐AD

In 1777, French soldier Marquis de Lafayette came to America to help the colonists fight Great Britain in the American Revolutionary War (1775–1783). Lafayette believed that slavery was inconsistent with America's ideals of liberty and freedom. In 1821, he wrote to former U.S. president Thomas Jefferson, "Are you sure, my dear friend, that extending the principle of slavery to the new raised states is a method to facilitate [assist] the means of getting rid of it? I would have thought that by spreading the prejudices, habits, and calculations of planters over a larger surface you rather increase the difficulties of final liberation [freedom]."

The Quakers, shown above at a meeting, are a religious group that began in England in the mid-17th century.

opposite of the concepts of independence and freedom upon which the United States had been founded.

One early abolitionist was Sojourner Truth. She was born a slave in New York (when slavery was still legal there) but escaped with her daughter. She was a Christian and believed God called her to preach against injustice. She made it her life's work to travel the country and speak out against slavery and in favor of women's rights.

The Workings of the Railroad

People who were a part of the Underground Railroad developed a secret code of words and terms to describe the participants and safe places. People who guided slaves from one place to another were called conductors. Locations where slaves would be safe were called stations or safe houses. People who hid escaped slaves were called stationmasters. The routes between stations were called lines. Slaves who were traveling with a conductor or staying with a stationmaster were known as cargo or freight.

The Ohio River was called the River Jordan, a reference to a river that appears in the Bible. Canada, which is north of the United States and provided safety to slaves, was known as the Promised Land.

Taking a Chance

One of the best-known conductors on the Underground Railroad was Harriet Tubman. William Lloyd Garrison, a well-known abolitionist, nicknamed her Moses after the prophet in the Bible who helped lead the Hebrew people

The road to freedom along the Underground Railroad was filled with dangers.

Harriet Tubman

Harriet Tubman was born a slave in Maryland, and she suffered numerous beatings. Once, she tried to defend a fellow slave and was hit in the head with a heavy object. The injury affected her for the rest of her life, causing her to fall into deep "spells." Tubman plotted her escape and finally succeeded with the help of the Underground Railroad. In 10 years, she made about 19 trips to the South and helped more than 300 people, including her family, to freedom. During the Civil War, Tubman worked for the Union as a cook, a nurse, and a spy.

out of slavery in Egypt. Tubman had many tricks to help slaves escape. For instance, she sometimes stole the master's horse and buggy to use on the first part of the trip. Another strategy was to leave on a Saturday night. Since newspapers weren't published on Sunday, the names of the escaped slaves would not be known until Monday, giving them a chance to get farther away from their owners.

Tubman once boasted that she "never lost a single passenger" on the Underground Railroad. She encouraged her cargo to keep moving on their journey, even if they were tired or scared. She reportedly would wave her gun at them and say, "You'll be free or die."

Escaping from slavery, or helping someone escape, was risky and dangerous. It was illegal to help slaves escape. Slave hunters could come to the North and force

Harriet Tubman (far left) guided members of her family and hundreds of other slaves to freedom in the North.

slaves back to their owners. Also, the Fugitive Slave Act made assisting or hiding slaves a **federal** crime. People who participated in the Underground Railroad could be sent to jail or fined as much as $500 (equal to approximately $10,000 today).

A FIRSTHAND LOOK AT
"GO DOWN, MOSES"

One of the gospel songs that inspired slaves on their path to freedom was "Go Down, Moses," written by Harry Thacker Burleigh. A 1917 version of the sheet music is housed at the Library of Congress. See page 60 for a link to view the sheet music of the song.

CHAPTER 2

WHAT AN ESCAPE WAS LIKE

Runaway slaves risked harsh punishments if they were captured.

EVERY JOURNEY ON THE
Underground Railroad had to be kept absolutely
secret. Once a slave decided he or she was ready
to make the trip, the first step was contacting
people who could help. Sometimes the conductors
approached slaves who seemed to be ready to
escape. Everyone involved had to be certain they
spoke only to people they could trust. One word
to the wrong person could ruin the plans and
cause serious problems for those who were caught
escaping or helping.

Slaves were bought and sold throughout the Americas at slave markets, such as this one in Virginia.

Moving from Station to Station

The average distance between stations was 10 to 15 miles (16 to 24 kilometers). At the time, most people traveled on foot. For slaves seeking freedom, this meant walking hundreds of miles from the South to the

A FIRSTHAND LOOK AT
A REWARD POSTER

Slaves were valuable property to their masters, and an escaped slave meant a loss of money. Owners did everything in their power to retrieve escaped slaves, often offering rewards for their return. Rewards were announced on posters, called broadsides, which were hung in public places. Some of these posters are housed at the Library of Congress in Washington, D.C. See page 60 for a link to view an original reward poster from 1847.

North. Some slaves also managed to travel by horse, boat, wagon, or train. They moved mostly at night and frequently wore disguises or carried papers giving them false identities. They would often head out in the dark with nothing but the stars to guide them. The slaves and their conductors feared barking dogs and slave masters making their evening rounds. But the escapees kept moving, staying quiet and heading for safety.

The farther north the fugitives traveled, the closer together the stations were. At each station, the exhausted slaves were given food, perhaps a change of clothes, and a place to rest. The Underground Railroad stretched for thousands of miles. From Kentucky and Virginia, the lines spread across Ohio and Indiana. From Maryland, the lines crossed Pennsylvania, and into New York and New England.

Slaves attempted to escape by any means possible, including by foot, boat, horseback, train, or wagon.

Traveling at night, though safer than daytime travel, was no guarantee that a slave would reach freedom.

Making the Journey

Most people on the Underground Railroad faced a long journey filled with uncertainty and fear. They knew they might not reach their goal, and if captured, they would be returned to their owners and be severely punished.

Some people thought that winter was the best time of year to escape. The cold weather would freeze the Ohio River, making it easier to cross. But the winter snow and ice made traveling north much slower and more difficult.

Although many conductors were experienced and trustworthy, slaves had a hard time knowing which situations were safe and which potentially were not. They often went days or weeks between stations, and they were always at risk of being found. Slave hunters rode horses and used bloodhounds to track the escapees, so frightened slaves often were at a disadvantage.

The Drinking Gourd

According to legend, "Follow the Drinking Gourd" was a song that many people on the Underground Railroad sang. Its lyrics helped escaped slaves find their way along the journey to the North.

> When the sun comes back and the first quail calls,
> Follow the Drinking Gourd.
> For the old man is waiting for to carry you to freedom,
> If you follow the Drinking Gourd.
>
> The riverbank makes a very good road,
> The dead trees show you the way,
> Left foot, peg foot, traveling on
> Follow the Drinking Gourd.
>
> The river ends between two hills,
> Follow the Drinking Gourd.
> There's another river on the other side,
> Follow the Drinking Gourd.
>
> Where the great river meets the little river,
> Follow the Drinking Gourd.
> For the old man is awaiting to carry you to freedom if you
> Follow the Drinking Gourd.

Frederick Douglass

Frederick Douglass was born a slave in Maryland. He escaped to the North by taking a train, a steamboat, and then another train. He became a leader of the abolitionist movement, as well as a talented writer and public speaker. Douglass wrote several books about his experiences as a slave and on the Underground Railroad. Among these are *Narrative of the Life of Frederick Douglass* and *My Bondage and My Freedom*.

Douglass opened his home in Rochester, New York, to many escaped slaves as they made their way to Canada. Douglass also worked to help African Americans receive educations and to help women gain the right to vote.

A drinking gourd is a hollowed-out squash or pumpkin that people used to scoop up water. For passengers on the Underground Railroad, the drinking gourd was also a reference to the Big Dipper, a constellation in the sky. The upper right star of the bowl of this constellation points toward the North Star. This helped passengers determine direction.

According to some stories, a sailor named Peg Leg Joe wrote the song. He would visit plantations and teach the song to slaves, encouraging them to escape to freedom. Historians are not sure if Peg Leg Joe was a real person or a combination of many people who helped on the Underground Railroad.

The Risks of Escape

Many escaped slaves did not make it to freedom. By some estimates, nearly four million slaves lived in the South, but only about 100,000 of them escaped slavery through the Underground Railroad. Some became sick on their journey and could not continue on. Slave hunters caught others. Many simply gave up. Even those who were not successful passed on their knowledge to others. They told other slaves about the safe routes and who along the routes could be trusted. The Underground Railroad endured.

YESTERDAY'S HEADLINES

THE NORTH STAR.

In 1847, Frederick Douglass began publishing a newspaper called the *North Star*. In the article "Our Paper and Its Prospects," Douglass explained the role of the publication:

We are now about to assume the management of the editorial department of a newspaper, devoted to the cause of Liberty, Humanity and Progress. . . . It has long been our anxious wish to see, in this slave-holding, slave-trading, and Negro-hating land, a printing-press and paper, permanently established, under the complete control and direction of the immediate victims of slavery and oppression.

CHAPTER 3

RIDING THE UNDERGROUND RAILROAD

The escape to freedom was especially dangerous for mothers with young children.

THE PEOPLE WHO ESCAPED ON the Underground Railroad were young and old, male and female, and from many different states. Healthy men made up the majority of the escapees. Women with children had a harder time with the journey. Older people often could not manage the miles of walking and other physical challenges of the trip.

Slaves worked the fields from 10 to 18 hours a day in the hot and humid weather of the South.

Making the Decision

Many slaves decided to escape because they could no longer suffer the beatings and long, backbreaking hours of physical labor. They could not face living in tiny shacks and eating a poor diet. As frightening as the journey might be, many slaves believed that it could be no worse than the hardships they experienced on a daily basis.

Some slaves decided to flee because they knew they were about to be sold. If an owner suddenly sold some or all of his slaves, family members could be separated and slaves would become the property of a new owner. Jacob Blockson, a slave from Delaware, explained, "I made up my mind that I did not want to be sold like a horse. . . . I resolved to die sooner than I would be taken back."

Other slaves were afraid to leave. They had become so accustomed to serving their masters that they did

A reward poster from an 1838 newspaper offers $150 for the capture of Henry May, "a first rate dining-room servant."

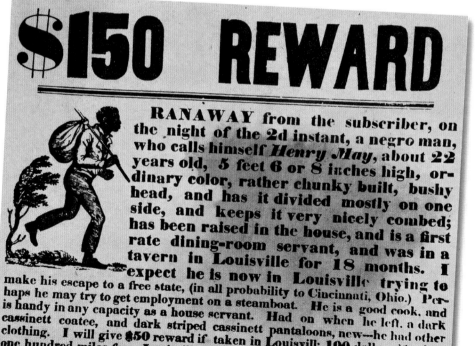

$150 REWARD

RANAWAY from the subscriber, on the night of the 2d instant, a negro man, who calls himself *Henry May*, about 22 years old, 5 feet 6 or 8 inches high, ordinary color, rather chunky built, bushy head, and has it divided mostly on one side, and keeps it very nicely combed; has been raised in the house, and is a first rate dining-room servant, and was in a tavern in Louisville for 18 months. I expect he is now in Louisville trying to make his escape to a free state, (in all probability to Cincinnati, Ohio.) Perhaps he may try to get employment on a steamboat. He is a good cook, and is handy in any capacity as a house servant. Had on when he left, a dark cassinett coatee, and dark striped cassinett pantaloons, new—he had other clothing. I will give $50 reward if taken in Louisvill; 100 dollars if taken one hundred miles from Louisville in this State, and 150 dollars if taken out of this State, and delivered to me, or secured in any jail so that I can get him again.

Bardstown, Ky., September 3d, 1838.   WILLIAM BURKE.

not dare to think of another way of living. Some feared being caught and punished, and others did not want to leave behind family members who could not make the trip.

Keeping a Record

William Green was a slave from Maryland who escaped on the Underground Railroad. He wrote the story of his escape in 1853 in a book called *Narrative of Events in the Life of William Green (Formerly a Slave)*. He described how he and his group traveled on foot for two days. Then a Quaker man let them stay at his home. The man fed them and gave them directions for the rest of their journey. Green and the others walked for several more days and stayed in

Maria Weems disguised herself as a man to escape. She journeyed from slavery in Maryland to freedom in Philadelphia and Canada.

Armed fugitive slave families defended themselves against slave catchers.

A FIRSTHAND LOOK AT
THE LIFE OF WILLIAM GREEN

William Green's book, *Narrative of Events in the Life of William Green (Formerly a Slave)*, is an insightful look into a slave's life from birth to freedom. Green comments on the "blighting [harmful] effects of Slavery" and on the Fugitive Slave Act. The book ends with an antislavery poem entitled "Anti-Slavery Song," which Green probably wrote. See page 60 for a link to view the book and read its entire contents.

Other versions of underground railroads have been used all over the world. In Asia, people who flee from the brutal dictatorship of North Korea try to travel through a network in China to a Southeast Asian nation that will let them live in freedom. An organization in Michigan called Underground Railroad, Inc., helps women who are victims of violence, providing shelter for them and their children. The idea of helping runaway slaves more than 150 years ago continues to inspire people today.

another home. Then a conductor put them on a boat to Philadelphia. From there, they rode a boat to New York. They finally settled in Springfield, Massachusetts.

J. W. C. Pennington was another escapee from Maryland. He wrote about his journey to freedom in *The Fugitive Blacksmith*. William Still kept a diary of his experiences on the Underground Railroad. Still was a free black man who opened his Philadelphia home as a station for fugitives. His was one of the busiest stations in the East. His memories were published in 1872 as *The Underground Rail Road: A Record of Facts,*

Authentic Narratives, Letters, &c. Narrating the Hardships, Hair-Breadth Escapes, and Death Struggles of the Slaves in Their Efforts for Freedom.

Using Imagination

Some slaves used imaginative means to get to safety. One of the most famous stories is of Henry Brown, a slave in Virginia. He asked a free black man to make a box for him. The box was only 3 feet (0.9 meter) long,

Henry Brown, nicknamed Box, outwitted his owners by escaping to freedom in a crate shipped from Maryland to Philadelphia.

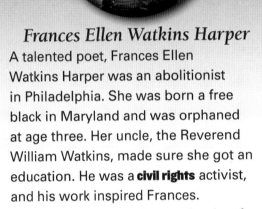

Frances Ellen Watkins Harper

A talented poet, Frances Ellen Watkins Harper was an abolitionist in Philadelphia. She was born a free black in Maryland and was orphaned at age three. Her uncle, the Reverend William Watkins, made sure she got an education. He was a **civil rights** activist, and his work inspired Frances.

Frances published many books of poetry about slavery, and she gave speeches about her abolitionist beliefs. She opened her home as a station on the Underground Railroad and helped pay for Underground Railroad expenses with the profits from her books. Harper also worked for women's rights.

2 feet (0.6 m) wide, and 2.5 feet (0.75 m) deep. The box had airholes drilled into it. Brown sent a secret message to the Philadelphia Anti-Slavery Office, telling people there to look out for a crate and to open it right away. Brown got in the box with some food and water. A friendly local white man, Samuel Smith, took the box to the Richmond, Virginia, train station, and it was shipped north. Brown survived the bumpy journey, and abolitionist Lucretia Mott welcomed him to her home, a station on the Underground Railroad. Samuel Smith, however, was arrested after shipping two other slaves and was sent to jail for eight years.

Ellen Craft's light complexion allowed her to pass as a white woman as she and her husband traveled to Philadelphia.

Another story involves husband and wife William and Ellen Craft. They were both slaves in Georgia, but Ellen had very light skin and could pass for white. She dressed up as a man and pretended that William was her slave. They traveled by train, steamboat, and ferry, before arriving in Philadelphia. There, William Lloyd Garrison, William Wells Brown, and other abolitionists offered them assistance.

THE NETWORK OF FREEDOM SITES

Many Underground Railroad escape routes were located along the Ohio River.

THROUGHOUT THE NORTH,

there were dozens of towns and cities with connections to the Underground Railroad. Many of them were located in an area called the Borderland, a region along the border between free states and slave states. The Ohio River was an important part of that border. Ohio cities such as Cincinnati, Ripley, and Oxford were very active in the Underground Railroad. So were the Indiana cities of Richmond, Newport (now Fountain City), and Madison.

Many slaves, such as these shown crossing the Rappahannock River in Virginia, escaped during the American Civil War.

Other Active Cities on the Railroad

Many escaped slaves also reached safety in the Chesapeake Bay area, including cities such as Philadelphia, Pennsylvania, and Baltimore, Maryland. Farther north, slaves also settled in Detroit, Michigan; Boston, Massachusetts; and Niagara Falls and Rochester, New York.

Although some fugitive slaves settled in Northern cities, others chose to continue northward to Canada. In Canada, slavery was illegal, and there was no risk of being captured. The Fugitive Slave Act had no power in another country. The Canadian province of Ontario was home to as many as 17,000 former slaves, who arrived from areas such as Ohio and New York.

Stops on the Underground Railroad

As they traveled the Underground Railroad, many escaped slaves stayed in people's homes. Often the stationmasters had a signal, such as a lit lantern, which told people their home was safe.

In Tabor, Iowa, the home of minister John Todd was an important station. This two-story clapboard house gave many people a place to stay on their journey. In

John Rankin

John Rankin was a Presbyterian minister and an active stationmaster. While living in Ripley, Ohio, he often wrote letters to the local newspaper, voicing his opposition to slavery. He also published *Letters on American Slavery,* a collection of letters he had written to his slave-owning brother in Virginia. He eventually influenced his brother to sell his slaves. William Lloyd Garrison published Rankin's collection of letters in his newspaper, the *Liberator.* Rankin's home sat high above the town of Ripley. He was able to signal slaves when it was clear to approach, and he offered shelter to thousands of fugitives.

Sometimes escaped slaves would build temporary shelters on their journey to freedom.

Lewis, Iowa, Reverend George B. Hitchcock welcomed slaves to his two-story brick home.

The Bethel African Methodist Episcopal (AME) Church in Indianapolis, Indiana, and the St. James AME Zion Church in Ithaca, New York, were important stations. Both churches provided a place for slaves who were going to Canada.

Oakdale is the name of a home in Chadds Ford, Pennsylvania, that was the first Underground Railroad stop north of Delaware. It had a secret square room, located between a walk-in fireplace and a carriage house wall, where slaves were allowed to stay. Another stop in Pennsylvania was White Horse Farm in Schuylkill Township. Its owner, Elijah Pennypacker, was a member of the House of Representatives. He personally transported slaves from his home to points north.

Throughout the United States, there were dozens of other stops on the railroad. But not all stations were homes and churches. Slaves often used barns or empty sheds as places to sleep for the night. They sometimes even used caves or swamps.

Runaway slaves arrived at Underground Railroad stations carrying few, if any, possessions.

Grand Central Station

Levi Coffin was a Quaker who strongly opposed slavery. He and his wife, Catherine White Coffin, were very active in the Underground Railroad in Ohio and Indiana. Their home in Newport, Indiana, was known as the Grand Central Station of the Underground Railroad. Coffin's success as a merchant and business leader allowed him to help finance Underground Railroad activities. Coffin received death threats because of his work as an abolitionist. At one point, some customers refused to shop in his store. As Indiana grew, however, more antislavery supporters moved in, and he received their encouragement.

The Coffins built their house in Newport, Indiana, specifically to hide runaway slaves. The house had several secret rooms and stairways.

Levi Coffi
Hou

During the years they lived in Newport, Indiana, Levi and Catherine White Coffin helped about 2,000 slaves reach freedom.

In 1847, the Coffins moved to Cincinnati, which had a strong network of Underground Railroad stations, but they kept their Newport home available as a safe house.

A FIRSTHAND LOOK AT
JOHN RANKIN'S HOUSE

John Rankin's house in Ripley, Ohio, was once an important safe house on the Underground Railroad. It is now a museum and is listed as a U.S. National Historic Landmark. See page 60 for a link to view the National Park Service's site about the house and a link to view photographs of the home's interior, much as it appeared in the mid-19th century.

Underground Railroad lines crisscrossed Ohio and Indiana, providing routes to freedom.

More Places to Find Shelter

Some slaves in Virginia and North Carolina settled in the Great Dismal Swamp. This area covers 1,000 square miles (2,600 square km) along the border of the two states. The dense plant life made the swamp a good hiding spot, and slave hunters had difficulty traveling through it. The Great Dismal Swamp was a Maroon community, a permanent settlement of fugitive slaves. Many Maroon communities formed in areas of thick forests and swamps in the South.

John Rankin hid runaway slaves in a secret place under the floor of the wooden back porch of his house in Ripley, Ohio.

Early in American colonial history, Spanish and Native American communities controlled some areas that are now part of the United States. Some slaves were able to escape and find help in these areas. Some slaves escaped to Fort Mose near St. Augustine, Florida, which was then controlled by the Spanish. Others joined Seminole populations elsewhere in Florida. Even later, after Florida became a U.S. territory, many slaves did not go north. Instead, they escaped south to regions that had once been controlled by Spain. Others made their way to parts of the American West, Mexico, the Caribbean Islands, and South America.

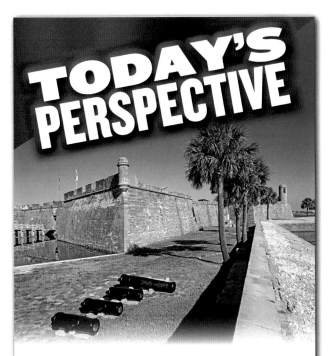

TODAY'S PERSPECTIVE

Founded in 1565 by Spanish colonists, St. Augustine (above) was the first permanent European settlement in North America. Fort Mose, located just north of St. Augustine, was established in 1738. It was the first free black community in what would become the United States. Fort Mose welcomed escaped slaves from South Carolina and Georgia even before the Underground Railroad formed. Florida became a U.S. territory in 1822 and a state in 1845.

THE CIVIL WAR AND THE END OF SLAVERY

The issue of slavery was one of the reasons for the Civil War.

BY THE MID–1800S, ARGUMENTS over the issue of slavery had reached a boiling point. Many people in the North were opposed to the practice and wanted it abolished. Many Southern landowners, however, saw slave ownership as a right guaranteed to them by their states. As the debate over states' rights continued, tempers grew more heated. Soon the country would divide, pitting the North against the South, in the American Civil War.

Federal law said that runaway slaves must be returned to their owners, even if they were found in Northern states.

Secession from the Union

In 1848, the United States acquired a great deal of land in the West. People wondered whether the new territories would allow slavery. Eventually, as part of the **Compromise** of 1850, California entered the Union as a free state. The territories of Arizona, Utah, Nevada, and New Mexico were given the right to allow slavery if they chose to. This was an attempt to keep the free states and slave states balanced, but few people were happy with the compromise.

Another part of the compromise was the second Fugitive Slave Act, which also passed in 1850. This law was even more powerful than the first one. It stated that any official who did not arrest and return a runaway slave could be jailed or fined $1,000 (equal to $20,000 today). The Southern states were angry that abolitionists were helping slaves escape. The Northern states were angry that slave hunters were trying to invade their homes, looking for fugitives.

Finally, in December 1860, South Carolina seceded, or left, the Union. Other Southern states soon followed. The seceded states formed the Confederate States of America, or Confederacy, which had a new and totally separate government. Jefferson Davis was elected its president.

Harriet Beecher Stowe

An abolitionist and an author, Harriet Beecher Stowe is best remembered for writing *Uncle Tom's Cabin*. This book tells the story of Eliza, a slave who escapes with her son, and Uncle Tom, a slave who is sold to the cruel Simon Legree. Published in 1852, the novel received attention throughout the United States and the world. Some people say that the book contributed to the outbreak of the Civil War. Some sources claim that President Abraham Lincoln once called Stowe "the little woman who wrote the book that started this great war." She and her husband opened their home in Cincinnati as a station on the Underground Railroad.

A Nation Divided

President Abraham Lincoln, who had been elected in 1860, faced difficult challenges. Many people wanted him to end slavery, but he thought the process should be a gradual one. He took office in March 1861, and just one month later, the Civil War began.

For the next four years, soldiers from the North and South faced one another on the battlefield. Young men left farms in the South and factories in the North, and fought in terrible conditions throughout the country. Many soldiers died of disease. The Union was better

The Civil War was a long, bloody conflict.

The Emancipation Proclamation freed all slaves in Confederate states that were still fighting the Union. Here, freed slaves join Union troops in New Bern, North Carolina.

prepared for war, with more than 1.5 million soldiers, including some 180,000 black soldiers. The Confederacy had a total of roughly 900,000 soldiers.

In the end, more than 600,000 soldiers died in the Civil War. The North defeated the South, and the Southern states eventually rejoined the Union.

YESTERDAY'S HEADLINES

On April 14, 1865, five days after the Civil War officially ended, President Lincoln was shot while attending a performance at Ford's Theatre in Washington, D.C. John Wilkes Booth, a Confederate supporter, shot the president during a break in the play. Lincoln died the next day.

The *National News* reported the **assassination** with the headline "Lincoln Shot— Condition Considered Hopeless—Will Not Live Through Night, Doctors Declare." The paper reported, "Our president's life was taken at a time of new beginnings for him and for us. It was a time of renewed promise for the nation."

The End of Slavery

On January 1, 1863, President Lincoln issued the Emancipation Proclamation. This order immediately freed 50,000 slaves. The remaining slaves in the Confederate states were freed when Union soldiers took control of those areas. The proclamation did not free the slaves in the Union states of Delaware, Kentucky, West Virginia, Missouri, and Maryland. But Missouri and Maryland outlawed slavery in their states themselves.

The Emancipation Proclamation sent a message all over the world that the United States would no longer tolerate slavery. The proclamation also set the stage for the 13th **Amendment** to the U.S. Constitution. This amendment was **ratified** in 1865, officially abolishing slavery in all U.S. states and territories.

The war was over, and slavery was illegal. The Underground Railroad had served its purpose.

This U.S. postage stamp was issued in 1940 to celebrate the 75th anniversary of the 13th Amendment, which outlawed slavery in the United States.

A FIRSTHAND LOOK AT
THE 13TH AMENDMENT

Congress passed the 13th Amendment on January 31, 1865, and it was ratified on December 6 of the same year. This amendment officially abolished slavery and marked the beginning of the long struggle for civil rights in the United States. See page 60 for a link to view the original proposal for the amendment, which is signed by President Lincoln.

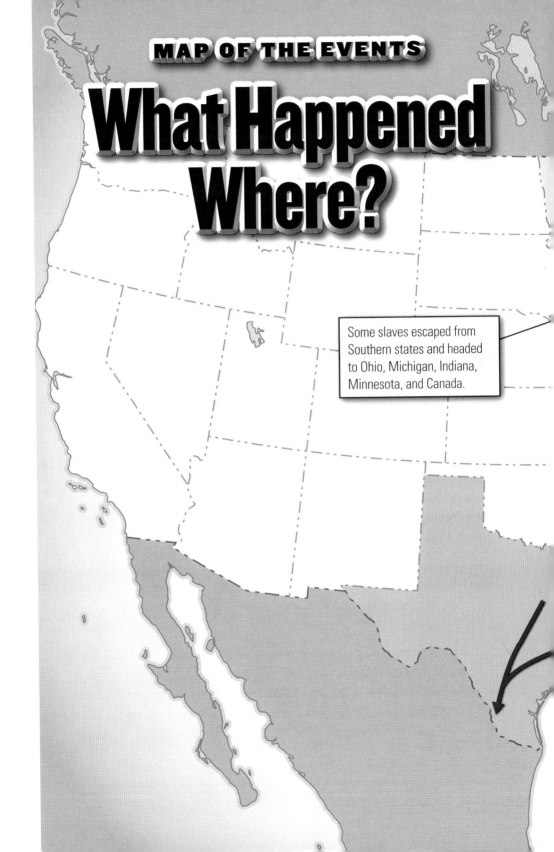

What Happened Where?

Some slaves escaped from Southern states and headed to Ohio, Michigan, Indiana, Minnesota, and Canada.

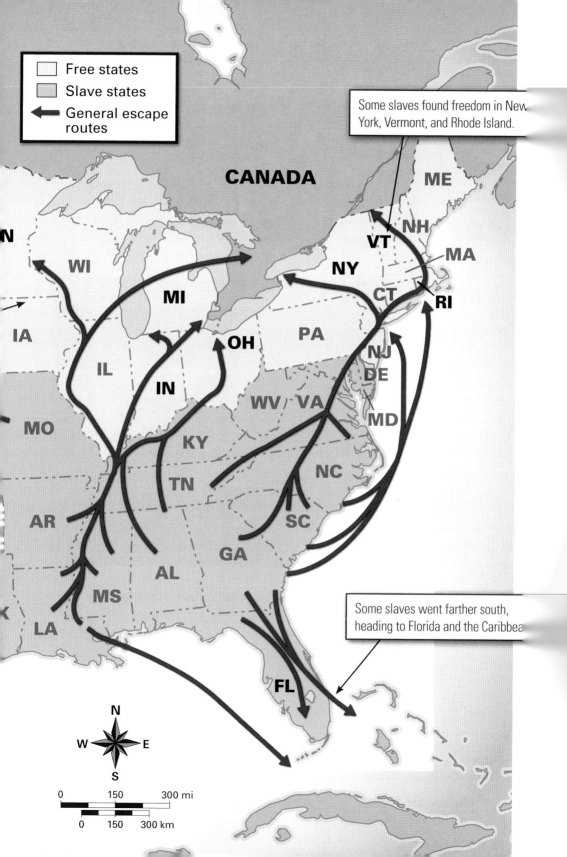

Free states

Slave states

General escape routes

Some slaves found freedom in New York, Vermont, and Rhode Island.

Some slaves went farther south, heading to Florida and the Caribbean

CANADA

ME

NH

VT

MA

NY

CT

RI

MN

WI

MI

IA

IL

IN

OH

PA

NJ

DE

MO

KY

WV

VA

MD

TN

NC

AR

SC

GA

AL

NC

MS

LA

FL

N

W   E

S

0   150   300 mi

0   150   300 km

Slavery and Civil Rights Today

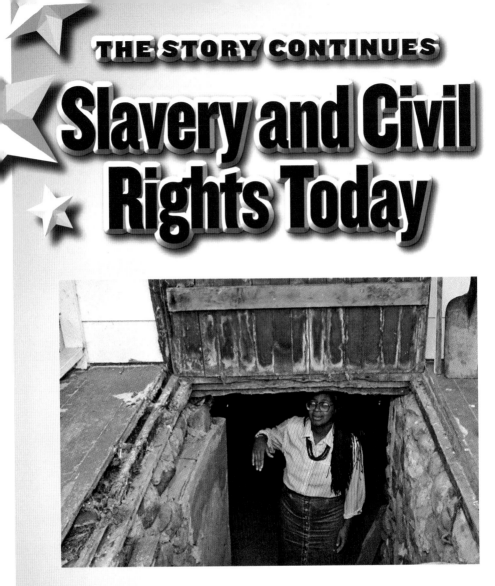

This hidden staircase at an Underground Railroad station is a reminder of African Americans' struggle for freedom during the many years of slavery in the United States.

In 1870, the 15th Amendment to the U.S. Constitution gave voting rights to men of all races. Several southern states, however, restricted these rights by giving black citizens unfair tests before they voted. In some places, a **poll tax** had to be paid in order for a black citizen to vote.

Many inequalities still existed in the United States. After the Civil War, southern states began passing laws requiring **segregation**. Separate areas were created for black Americans and white Americans.

In 1954, the Supreme Court ruled that separate public schools for blacks and whites were unconstitutional. As legal segregation began to end, however, tension increased. Black students were threatened, and many had to have the protection of armed U.S. soldiers simply to enter their schools.

On August 28, 1963, civil rights leader Martin Luther King Jr. gave his famous "I Have a Dream" speech in which he talked about the inequalities that African Americans still faced. King's powerful words contributed to the passage of the Civil Rights Act of 1964.

Slavery still exists in many parts of the world. In India, some young children, called "carpet slaves," are locked in rooms and weave rugs for hours on end. Young girls are sold like property in Thailand, and thousands of slaves are bought and sold in Sudan.

The Underground Railroad helped thousands of enslaved people escape to freedom. It was a triumph of human will and spirit. Perhaps there will be a day when slavery is abolished throughout the world, and all people can experience liberty and freedom.

INFLUENTIAL INDIVIDUALS

Benjamin Franklin (1706–1790) was one of the founders of the United States. He was a politician, writer, inventor, and abolitionist.

Marquis de Lafayette (1757–1834) was a French military officer who fought against the British in the American Revolutionary War. He expressed his disapproval of the U.S. practice of slavery.

Lucretia Mott (1793–1880) was a Quaker who worked for abolition, social reform, and women's rights. She and her husband founded the Pennsylvania Anti-Slavery Society.

John Rankin

John Rankin (1793–1886) was a Presbyterian minister and abolitionist. He wrote *Letters on American Slavery* and was one of the most active stationmasters on the Underground Railroad.

Sojourner Truth (c.1797–1883) was born a slave in New York and later escaped to freedom. She traveled the country, speaking about abolition and women's rights.

Levi Coffin (1798–1877) was an abolitionist and a businessman. A Quaker, he opened his Indiana and Ohio homes to fugitives, and was sometimes called the President of the Underground Railroad.

Levi Coffin

William Lloyd Garrison (1805–1879) was an abolitionist who published the antislavery newspaper the *Liberator*. He was critical of the U.S. Constitution because it did not prevent the practice of slavery.

William Green (?–?) was a slave who escaped his master in Maryland and journeyed north. He published his book, *Narrative of Events in the Life of William Green (Formerly a Slave)*, in 1853.

Abraham Lincoln (1809–1865) served as the 16th president of the United States. He issued the Emancipation Proclamation and pushed for the 13th Amendment. He was assassinated five days after the Civil War ended.

J. W. C. Pennington (1809–1871) was an escaped slave who recorded his journey in *The Fugitive Blacksmith*.

Harriet Beecher Stowe (1811–1896) was an abolitionist and an author. She is best remembered for writing *Uncle Tom's Cabin*, a novel that may have contributed to the beginning of the Civil War.

William Wells Brown (1814–1884) was born into slavery but escaped to the North. He became a well-known abolitionist, novelist, and historian.

Frederick Douglass (1817–1895) was a writer, speaker, and abolitionist leader.

Harriet Tubman (1820–1913) was a slave who escaped and made her way to the North. After her escape, she made many return trips, helping more than 300 slaves to freedom.

Harriet Tubman

Frances Ellen Watkins Harper (1825–1911) was a poet and abolitionist.

TIMELINE

1619

The first slaves are brought to Jamestown, Virginia, in the American colonies.

1738

Fort Mose becomes the first free black community in what would become the United States.

1775

The world's first abolitionist society is founded in Philadelphia; Benjamin Franklin becomes its president in 1787.

1860

Abraham Lincoln is elected president of the United States.

1861-1865

The Union and the Confederacy fight in the Civil War.

1863

The Emancipation Proclamation is issued.

The first Fugitive Slave Act is passed, outlawing efforts to help runaway slaves.

1808

The United States bans the trade of slaves from Africa, but it continues illegally.

1850

The second Fugitive Slave Act is passed, which is much harsher than the first; California enters the Union as a free state.

1865

The 13th Amendment is passed, outlawing slavery throughout the United States.

UNITED STATES OF AMERICA

EMANCIPATION

75TH ANNIVERSARY OF THE 13TH AMENDMENT TO THE CONSTITUTION

POSTAGE 3 CENTS

LIVING HISTORY

Primary sources provide firsthand evidence about a topic. Witnesses to a historical event create primary sources. They include autobiographies, newspaper reports of the time, oral histories, photographs, and memoirs. A secondary source analyzes primary sources, and is one step or more removed from the event. Secondary sources include textbooks, encyclopedias, and commentaries.

"Go Down, Moses" To view the sheet music to the gospel song "Go Down, Moses," written by Harry Thacker Burleigh, go to *www.americaslibrary.gov/aa/tubman/aa_tubman_rail_2_e.html*

John Rankin's House To view photographs of the interior of John Rankin's safe house in Ripley, Ohio, go to *www.colefurniture.com/gallery/rankin_house_ripley.htm*

To visit the National Park Service's site dedicated to the Rankin house, go to *www.nps.gov/nr/travel/underground/oh3.htm*

Reward Poster To view an 1847 reward poster offering $200 for the capture of a slave and his family, go to *www.americaslibrary.gov/aa/tubman/aa_tubman_rail_1_e.html*

The 13th Amendment To view the original proposal for the 13th Amendment, signed by President Abraham Lincoln, go to *www.archives.gov/historical-docs/document.html?doc=9&title.raw=13th%20Amendment%20to%20the%20U.S.%20Constitution%253A%20Abolition%20of%20Slavery*

William Green's Autobiography To view an original page of William Green's book, *Narrative of Events in the Life of William Green (Formerly a Slave),* and read its entire contents, go to *http://memory.loc.gov/cgi-bin/query/r?ammem/lhbcbbib:@OR%28@field%28AUTHOR+@3%28Green,+William,+former+slave++%29%29+@field%28OTHER+@3%28Green,+William,+former+slave++%29%29%29*

Books

Lantier, Patricia. *Harriet Tubman: Conductor on the Underground Railroad*. New York: Crabtree, 2010.

Lassieur, Allison. *The Underground Railroad: An Interactive History Adventure*. Minneapolis: Capstone Press, 2008.

Nolen, Jerdine. *Eliza's Freedom Road: An Underground Railroad Diary*. New York: Simon & Schuster Books for Young Readers, 2011.

Roop, Peter. *Who Conducted the Underground Railroad? And Other Questions About the Path to Freedom*. New York: Scholastic, 2008.

Rosenberg, Aaron. *The Civil War*. New York: Scholastic Paperbacks, 2011.

West, Terry. *Narrative of the Life of Frederick Douglass: A Graphic Classic Based on the Autobiography by Frederick Douglass*. New York: Scholastic, 2009.

Web Sites

National Geographic: The Underground Railroad
www.nationalgeographic.com/railroad/j1.html
This interactive site helps users understand the decisions and risks involved in the Underground Railroad.

National Park Service: Aboard the Underground Railroad
www.nps.gov/nr/travel/underground/
This site lists the many geographic sites that served as safe places throughout the Underground Railroad system.

National Underground Railroad Freedom Center
www.freedomcenter.org/
At this museum, visitors learn about slavery and how the Underground Railroad worked. The museum also features dramatic readings and activities, as well as information about modern-day slavery.

GLOSSARY

abolitionist (ab-uh-LISH-uh-nist) a person in favor of immediately ending slavery

amendment (uh-MEND-muhnt) a change made to a law or legal document

assassination (uh-sass-uh-NAY-shuhn) the murder of someone famous or important

civil rights (SIV-il RITES) the individual rights that all members of society have, including freedom and equal treatment under the law

compromise (KOM-pruh-mize) an agreement between two sides that requires each to give up something that it wants

federal (FED-ur-uhl) referring to a system of government that balances power between states and the national government; or, another name for the national government

fugitive (FYOO-juh-tiv) someone who is running away, usually in an illegal way

plantations (plan-TAY-shuhnz) large farms where crops such as cotton, tobacco, and coffee are grown

poll tax (POLE TACKS) a fee someone has to pay in order to vote

ratified (RAT-uh-fyed) agreed to or approved officially

segregation (seg-ruh-GAY-shuhn) the act of separating people based on race, gender, or other factors

U.S. Constitution (YOO ESS kahn-sti-TOO-shuhn) a document that contains the U.S. system of laws, including all the rights of the people and the responsibilities of the government

INDEX

Page numbers in *italics* indicate illustrations.

ABOUT THE AUTHOR

Lucia Raatma earned a bachelor's degree from the University of South Carolina and a master's degree from New York University. She has authored dozens of books for young readers and particularly enjoys writing about American history. She finds the Underground Railroad to be a fascinating subject, since it champions individual rights and the human spirit. For more information, *visit www.luciaraatma.com*